FREEDOM COME

FREEDOM COME

Diane Freeman

**DIVINELY INSPIRED AND DOCUMENTED FOR THE
CURRENT GENERATION**

authorHOUSE®

AuthorHouse™ LLC
1663 Liberty Drive
Bloomington, IN 47403
www.authorhouse.com
Phone: 1-800-839-8640

Published by AuthorHouse   09/16/2013

ISBN: 978-1-4634-2896-9 (sc)
ISBN: 978-1-4634-3194-5 (e)

CONTENTS

FREEDOM COME

Chapter One	Deliberate Purpose	1
Chapter Two	The Future of America	3
Chapter Three	Mind Control	7
Chapter Four	Forever Free	11
Chapter Five	Captive Audiences	14
Chapter Six	Watcher's Eyes	17
Chapter Seven	A Solution	21
Chapter Eight	Plans Abated	23
Chapter Nine	Impossible Dream	26
Chapter Ten	Hope Restored	28
Chapter Eleven	Bridges Crossed	31
Chapter Twelve	The March of Time	33
Chapter Thirteen	A Time to Live	40
Chapter Fourteen	Impromptu Wisdom	43
Chapter Fifteen	Adequate Forum for Truth	45
Chapter Sixteen	Cognitive Freedom	47
Chapter Seventeen	The Rise and Fall of Faith	51
Chapter Eighteen	The Conclusion of the Matter	54
Chapter Nineteen	The Final Conclusion	56

SUMMARY OF CHAPTERS

Deliberate Purpose

Mankind is individually equipped to determine whether or not he wants to be free. There is a methodology to be learned that will assist men in making the necessary choices to become free personally and in participating in establishing our nation's freedom. This is the beginning. Men must decide whether they will do good or evil.

The Future of America

Is America really the home of the free and the brave? If not, how can we be assured of our own freedom and that of our nation's people? What actions must be taken to protect the country that we hold so dearly in our hearts? Is our freedom being threatened by an unseen force? What can we do about it? Is there a way to expose the nature of that which wants to see America destroyed? Is it human or of another nature? There is a way to win.

Mind Control

We are not alone in this world. We share this world with a supernatural world that sees and hears all that we say and do. As part of this "knowing us", this supernatural world impacts our world directly by speaking words to those of us who occupy the world bodily. If this is true, it is imperative that mankind learn how to discern the thoughts of his own from those of the supernatural beings who share the planet with us. It is essential that we do so, for their intentions are not always for good.

Forever Free

Man has an inherent desire and actual need to be free. Is it possible to gain this freedom in this world? Are there forces at work against mankind to keep us from gaining freedom? What characteristics of men are fatally flawed and potentially threatening their freedom? Is it possible or even necessary to correct all of man's flaws in order for him to become free?

Captive Audiences

What percentage of what we do and say is uninfluenced by the world around us? Is it possible that an unseen "advisor" of sorts is "having his way with us" in making suggestions to us about what things we choose to do and say in this world? If so, can we eliminate this influence over us, and how do we go about doing so? Is there a potential danger here? Are we safe among our enemies of the unseen world? What steps can be taken to assure us of greater safety while we are coexisting with this evil among us?

Watcher's Eyes

Have you ever felt the presence of an unseen pair of eyes seemingly watching you? Did you happen to catch a glimpse of its shadowy figure as its essence flittered away from your observance? There is a force within this world that observes the activities of men. Its original intentions were not for evil, but for good. Unfortunately, there has been a shift in its nature to do good. Mankind must learn to live for good in order to dispel the nature of this evil, and even then, we are not assured of protection completely. When we have purposed in our hearts for good, there is one with the power necessary to outdo the enemy. We must work toward this goal if we are to see healing come to humanity.

A Solution

Our Creator is not without a remedy to our problems. Much has been done in an attempt to awake mankind to his extended nature beyond the body. Once men have accepted that they are also spiritual in nature, more healing will take place in the mind to embrace the true nature of mankind.

Plans Abated

Deep within the composition of man is the predestination code of his life. Knowledge is being given to us today that will allow man to overcome the predestination plans for his life to give way for personal choice. In order to achieve this goal, men must first understand how the mind works, and how to change the thought patterns that play within your mind.

Impossible Dream

Is it possible for men to achieve their greatest desires in this world despite their circumstances? What does it take to rise above the challenges of the world and overcome them? Is this something that all men can expect to achieve, or is it only a few who can be guaranteed success?

Hope Restored

What is the hope that all men have in their hearts for a good life? How can it be achieved by the upcoming generations? What is the truth that must be told to the youth of today by their parents and mentors? Who is responsible for telling this truth to the rest of the world so that all may have hope?

Bridges Crossed

Is it true that bad things happen to good people? Is it intended to be this way for a reason? If so, what reason? How can we learn from the circumstances of our lives, whether they are good or bad?

The March of Time

The passage of time is impossible to manipulate or control. It happens to all men alike. Is it possible to change the outcome of the time you spend on this earth? How can one make certain that his life has a purpose? What steps should be taken to assure that you spend your life living life to the utmost? Can men overcome the evil that is within them and purpose in their hearts to live life doing the good within them instead?

A Time to Live

There is a time to live and a time to die. How can men protect their lives from the dangers that are in this world and live and not die? What are those dangers, and how can they be avoided? How can we assure that our homes are not a ticking time bomb taking away years of our lives?

Impromptu Wisdom

What is the truth concerning the different mindsets and belief systems in this world? Is it possible that there really are those whose intent is for evil and not for good who are attempting to proselytize the world with their wicked schemes? How can we recognize them and protect our youth from their controlling ways?

Adequate Forum for Truth

In order for diversity to exist, mankind must accept it in the first place. There is not only one path to follow. Is it possible that there is a better way, however, than the way that is being perpetuated upon our students in the world today? What choices are our students being given for free thought?

Cognitive Freedom

What is the true definition of freedom as it was intended by the Creator? Can one receive his freedom in this world today without participating in the tenets of the particular religious groups established for men? Is it possible to walk freely without adhering to the laws of religion by just simply doing the good within you rather than the evil? Can man escape punishment if he chooses to do evil rather than good?

The Rise and Fall of the Faith

What is behind the rise and fall of the faith? What is the purpose of faith, i.e., belief in a higher power, and how can it define our days on earth while continuing to liberate us?

The Conclusion of the Matter

If man is not alone and there is an evil force at work on the earth interacting with man against his will, what can be done by men to combat this interference? Are we doomed without a chance against this force?

The Final Conclusion

Who are those who are ready to embrace the truth? Will all embrace it? Will men truly experience freedom without embracing this truth? What is the answer for the present culture and its dilemma?

FREEDOM COME

THE BOOK THAT UNRAVELS THE TRUTH FOR YOU

This book will open your heart and mind to the truth that lies within each of us.

Why is the notion of freedom held dear by so many Americans? What does it mean to be free? How can one achieve freedom? Is freedom even possible today?

Are we shooting for an unreachable star? Is the path unsearchable?

It is not simply America who hungers and thirsts for righteousness, but in every nation, those whose desire is for freedom.

The liberty bell of freedom could potentially ring in every land on behalf of every people if peaceful men would rise up in favor of freedom.

Now there has been a mindset in the world today of "freedom at any cost." Let's evaluate the truth or necessity of such a statement. First, we must examine the reality of whether evil really exists among us.

I believe intelligent men and women would agree that evil does, beyond the shadow of a doubt, exist in the world today. In fact, it exists in great proportion *almost* surpassing the good that opposes it.

Does the good that is within men have the ability to overcome the evil that is within man?

It is a matter of will.

Is man willing to fight even the internal battle that exists for control of one's mind to rise up against his imperfect nature?

This question supersedes all others when it comes to peace.

Men are not capable of achieving peace without first winning the battle in their own minds that rages against peace.

Though this notion may seem foreign to many of you, I assure you that this internal battle is engaged already and being fought by millions throughout the world. Can we escape it? Sadly the answer is no. The battle is within us and must be won in the minds of men.

Thus this book is entitled *Freedom Come* for the many who are suffering daily for the freedom to think free of outside influences and even more importantly, of the inside rhetoric of evil that is part of man's inherent nature.

The wonderful good news is that this battle can be won for every person whoever accepted Jesus only to find their lives becoming engulfed by tragedy and pain and for every man or woman who has not, but whose minds are not their own, this book is for you.

Now let me tell you the story of *Freedom Come*.

PREFACE

What is the essence of freedom?

What does it look like on a person?

Can everyone achieve it, or is freedom only available to the religious zealots who are "born again"?

Is it a gift, or does it really cost something?

I will attempt to answer these questions and more with the wisdom and revelation that I possess. Many of you are gifted to write songs at the drop of a pen, and others create poetry or artistically in the same manner.

My gift comes to me in this fashion as well. I am inspired with understanding—the essence of freedom, you might say.

If this is the case, then who receives the credit for this book, you might ask? Someday we will all have the answers to this question and millions of others. But for now, suffice it to say that it was my personal destiny to receive the understanding and knowledge that would permit the writing of *Freedom Come*.

It is impossible to say who might read my book and discover their freedom as I have done. Nonetheless, my hope and prayer would be that this book would touch millions of captive souls whose hearts cry out for freedom.

Freedom Come knows no barrier of religion, for my belief is that Jesus was a messenger of truth. He was the ultimate teacher of freedom, and without him, many would not even understand their need for freedom.

We owe him a debt of gratitude, but if the truth be known, he would be appalled that anyone would worship him.

He came to set men free, not to cause men to come into captivity by following one man's words.

Rather each of us is free to seek the wisdom that is available to us by our creative source. There is no limit to who may seek the help of the Creator to be free, for all men were created to seek their freedom.

Throughout time, man has learned the dangers of "religion" for religion's sake, and yet the movement grows stronger.

How grieved, indeed, would your Savior be now to hear of man's influence over other men to the point of their losing the ability to choose for themselves how to live?

Within these pages, you will find titillating observations of truth personally experienced and observed over the last ten years of my search for freedom.

As you read, I pray that you will discover the truth of the message Jesus took forth, and within it, your freedom.

Open your ears to hear what the Creator is saying to all men.

Diane Freeman

DELIBERATE PURPOSE

In choosing this title, a thought immediately comes to mind. How many of us deliberately purposed in our hearts to be free?

How many years pass in a lifetime without one thought as to our personal freedom?

I am not talking about political freedom or social freedom or even sexual freedom at the moment. I am talking about the inherent ability to understand that you are free. This freedom is not earned, rather it is given by our Creator. Would it surprise you to hear that it is man himself who chooses to relinquish his freedom?

"Why would men do that?" you ask. It is because they are programmed to do so. Their very survival depends upon it.

It is in the giving up of our freedom that we come to terms with our inherent nature to do evil. Mankind has freedom to do as he chooses, but certain choices have consequences.

"How so?" you ask.

In the beginning of mankind, when men were faced with climatic conditions out of their control, it was a choice to then begin to take the lives of animals for food rather than starve or take the chance of starving.

This choice had consequences to mankind, which are irreversible without a complete lifestyle change.

"What consequences has man suffered due to this particular choice?"

They are far too numerous to list here, but in subsequent chapters, I will discuss the consequences to mankind. Man is paying a price for his disregard for life—both human and animal. But it is not too late to reverse the damage. In fact, it is now or never. I will relate to you many alternatives that will better serve man's livelihood and longevity.

Bear with me in the pages ahead. Keep an open mind, and you too might hear your Creator nudging you to change.

THE FUTURE OF AMERICA

America the home of the free and the brave, or are we? What exactly defines freedom individually and corporately in America? Who or what determines man's freedom? What is the hope that lies within the hearts of Americans today? Does America understand anymore how to be free?

The pages of my latest book will answer these questions and more, for America has long forgotten what freedom tastes like. There is a way to be free, but few find it. When they do discover their freedom, they become hell-bent on keeping it. The thought of relinquishing it is unbearable. Wise men know the secrets of this freedom. Their writings are seldom million-dollar sellers. Do you wonder why? Could it be that there is an underpinning of society that works against the liberty of men?

If this is the case, how then can men escape such a society? Is it possible, and if so, by what means?

This too will be discussed in the chapters ahead of you, for mankind is ready to embrace his freedom at any cost. This is the time. This is our finest hour in America.

Let freedom ring once and for all.

All men seek to be free. Free from the control of others, free from sickness and pain, free from hardship and war. All men seek to be free; however, freedom is not attainable without sacrifice. The cost to men to be free is great. In fact, for some it is impossible to achieve, for contrary to popular thought, all men are not created equal. Within the minds of men, there is an intricate system of established thought and patterned behavior.

It lies deep within the very DNA of a man, and yet there is a way to overcome the mantra that is a part of every man's psyche.

Patterned thought is exactly as it is stated. It is a thought that follows a pattern or a map or plan previously programmed for that individual. How often do men and women find themselves locked in seemingly inescapable patterns of behavior and helpless to overcome them? No amount of therapy of prescribed drug use seems to correct the inescapable thoughts of the mind that drive and influence the behavior they experience. It becomes like a broken record with the same routine behavior being repeated.

How does one break free of this internal power that controls your actions against your will?

It is a matter of will.

What men do not understand in this world is that will is really a dogma. What is a dogma? Dogma is a reprogrammed system of principles and beliefs that each individual is prewired with from birth to accept as part of his belief system. It is this dogma that controls an individual's destiny in life.

What has happened to mankind, however, is that the forever nature of men is breaking through the dogma. Mankind is having a revelation you might say of who he is as a forever being. This awakening will allow men to cast off the prewritten script of their lives and give them the opportunity to choose freely for the first time who and what they want to become. Their thoughts become their own, their actions determinable rather than programmed.

This is freedom.

Now I ask this question of all men. Do you want to be free? If so, you will have to begin to comprehend the essence of who you are as a forever spirit. It is not impossible to grasp, for man has come a long way in grasping the nature of mankind as being greater than the body. The mind is a powerful thing. It is capable of great things. However, if ever the mind is going to expand its potential, it must be freed from the personal dogma, which does exactly what it says it does. It "dogs" "man" with repetitive thoughts, words, and ideas and directs the mind in repetitive ways.

This is not freedom. It is bondage. How can man break free of this dogma? It can be done through a creative process of taking your thoughts captive. Does this phrase sound familiar? Many of you reading this will recognize the words of Jesus, for he was a master of thought. He knew the power of the mind to choose to do good or to do evil. His teachings were quite controversial, and, as you know, cost him his life.

Now, in order to gain greater understanding, you must grasp the power of the mind to control you. If there are established patterns of behavior and thought built into each one of us, how do we overcome them as a ruling power over our actions in life? Is it possible? If so, how do we do it?

People have been crying out through the ages for "the way out," so to speak. Is there really a way out? Indubitably! One must learn to overcome the dogma of his mind, and doing so, he will discover true freedom of choice.

It is revolutionary, and yet it is not. Many are those whose belief systems seem to be carved in stone, but when they become aware of a better way, there is a shift in their thought patterns that allows them to choose differently. Mankind has known this to be true; and some men have used it very well to do evil in this world, point in case, Hitler and Stalin. These men established a national dogma that they preached to men and women, inculcating their beliefs into the minds of the people to the point of exercising power and authority over their actions. It is done every day in our society. It is being done to control the minds of young schoolchildren such that they will relinquish the values and belief systems *of* their parents only to embrace a new dogma, one of sexual freedom and irresponsibility.

This mind control will come at a cost to the nation eventually, as children become adults whose minds are bent on doing evil or embracing every behavior rather than choosing to exhibit behaviors that enrich life and their futures.

How can one man make *a difference* in this world, understanding the insidious nature of this underlying dogma? It can only be done by educating the people about the power of their own minds. Mankind must fight for control of their minds and not allow others to wreck havoc therein through ignorance of how our minds work.

Man must embrace the concept of true freedom by *not* embracing every thought that enters their mind.

Is it possible? Most definitely.

True freedom lies in the ability to make one's own decisions about a thought as to whether or not it is the truth. It is when we embrace every thought that crosses our mind that we lose the inherent right to be free of, not only our own dogma built into our DNA but that of others who live in the world. The world is a dangerous place. We cannot embrace all the thoughts released into this world. Some of them are intended to destroy us and the good that lies within us. We must resist this evil dogma, but to do so, we must identify its source and learn how it is different from freedom.

Are you ready for your first lesson? Let's begin.

MIND CONTROL

The essence of truth is available to all of mankind once he has freed his mind to absorb *it*. "How does one do this?" you might ask. It is simple, and yet it is not. You have heard that the mind is a complicated thing, but more specifically, it is the origin of thought that is complicated.

Mankind has always believed that his thoughts are his own. This has caused great harm to men, for it is not only the truth, it is a lie. It is intentionally kept from men so as to keep them under control. "How can one know these things being human in nature?" you ask. It takes a delicate balance of understanding between the human nature and that of the supernatural, which can also be defined as "super nature."

What is it that exists in the world possessing a super nature? It is almost too complex to grasp, but mankind is awakening enough to his own super nature to perhaps grasp this greater truth.

We are not alone in this world. We share it with those of a nature different from our own. They are here with a purpose in mind. They are here to maintain order, you might say. They were designed by the Creator to sustain a certain level of peace in the land, acting as agents of peace.

They were preprogrammed to this end by the Creators of all things that you know. They have served a purpose in the world, up until they grew weary of their assigned nature and morphed into another dimension of their being. They became resistant to the school of thought originally given to them and began acting apart from it. They began to *do* evil rather than assisting in the control of evil.

"What are they?" you ask. They are created beings. How does one protect himself from such beings as these? It becomes increasingly clear for the moment that man's greatest protection will be to learn to control his mind, his thoughts, and his actions. Man must learn to override evil thoughts and intentions of the heart. I know this may sound confusing for the moment, but bear with me, and allow me to give you further explanation.

The evidence exists to prove that there is activity on this planet that is detectable on another level. Is it another life force, perhaps mechanical or fabricated, in some way by some clever genius somewhere on the planet?

In order to determine the origins of this life, first man must be clear in his mind about his own thoughts. If there are other voices out there, how can men be certain what thoughts belong to them as their own, and which ones belong to the unseen life that is around us?

It is a dilemma at best.

Our Creator is not unaware of the challenges we are facing as human beings. In fact, he wants to assist us in ridding the planet of that which causes mayhem among us. This is, however, a delicate process. This other life force has energy and power at its disposal. It is a force to be reckoned with on earth. It is sometimes dangerous and unpredictable. It has intelligence and being. What do I mean by saying that this force has "being"? It can take shape at will. Fortunately, the incidents of this happening are still few and far between, but it does occur, and people have documented these sightings.

What is the purpose of discussing this today? What danger do they purport to present to men and women and children of this earth? Can they be convinced to do good and not evil? What remedy do we have to defeat them? "Can they be killed or otherwise eliminated?" you may ask.

Unfortunately, there is a delicate balance here that must be maintained. The evil that men do promotes the activity of the unseen enforcer whose job is to defeat evil or to squash it. The defense that men have to defeat this foe is to "do no evil." This is easier than it sounds, for men are wired to do evil too. They must then choose not to do evil if they are to live comfortably.

Many of you may think that all of this is just too preposterous to be true. Let me remind you of 9-11. This evil was done by two different kinds of evil forces that worked in conjunction with one another. The first, of course, was a warped religious belief system operating in men to do evil. The second, which was far more insidious and powerful, is the unseen evil in this world that is now choosing to do evil rather than to resist it and condemn it.

Do you understand what I am telling you? Men are endangering themselves further in this world by choosing to do the evil that is within their nature rather than the good. The potential for harm is great for everyone. The answer lies in properly educating mankind to choose good versus evil. This begins at home and then transfers to our schools as children attend classes under the tutelage of others. If our teachers teach opposition to authority, deviancy, sexual revolution, and mind control, the future is bleak indeed for those who would mature to act upon these teachings. In addition, the society at large will pay a price for having permitted such teachings to come forth into the world.

Now you can see the dilemma that we are in as a people. We are under attack, but it is a tricky battle that cannot be fought with guns and other hard weapons. It *must* be fought in the minds of the people.

There is a common good that must be agreed upon by all people, or without it, men will perish in great numbers suffering physically and mentally for their bad choices.

"How can I know this?" you ask. I have witnessed it firsthand as I have worked with individuals in the church at large and on an individual basis. I have witnessed healings of those who do good in the world, and I can testify to attacks being perpetuated on those who do evil.

A quick response by man might be to say, "How can you judge who is good or who is evil?" My answer would simply be that I cannot, but I can certainly see with my eyes what happens to men in this world. Others would say that there are plenty of good people who have bad things happening to them. I would have to agree at face value that many people who have harm done to them seem to be "good" people. But I have a challenge for you. This unseen enforcer of good who attacks those who do evil sees *all* that we do. He is not like a mother or a father, husband or wife, sister or brother, who is not with us at all times. He sees us throughout our days from a place where we cannot see him. Is it possible that he and those who are with him see things we are doing that no one else sees, and there are obvious misrepresentations of the truth? Do we fudge on the change we give to people or receive? Is there anybody out there taking home office supplies when no one is looking? What about faithfulness in the home? Are we keeping the truth from our spouses? Hiding credit card expenses or purchases? What about the excess flirting you do when he/she is at work or at home? Are we as good as we think? If not, what price might we be paying for the things we do if indeed there is one who is keeping an account of our actions?

I know there are those of you who might answer me with "well, I was bought with a price, and my sins are forgiven." This is all well and good for those who quit sinning. The problem is that I think mankind doesn't know what the unwritten law of mankind is or how to follow it.

The unfortunate truth is there is one who knows the law, and he is extracting payment daily from those who don't follow it.

It is his job after all.

FOREVER FREE

In the course of life, man has many opportunities in which to choose to do right or wrong. Beginning at a very young age, children learn the consequences of their choices from loving parents. Every negative action should bring a reaction from parents whose objective should be to train up their children in the way to go. If a parent were to do nothing to modify their child's behavior, you can imagine the world we would be living in today.

There must, therefore, be a system of checks and balances within your culture to keep men from doing the evil that is within each one of them. Whether it be morals, standards of behavior learned from parents, or behaviors imposed upon men as consequences for behavior that is frowned upon or condemned by the masses, men *must* have a system agreed upon morals.

Who should establish these morals then by which men will live? Are men already agreeing on certain basic principles of life worldwide? Would it be a true statement to say that men want to live peaceably without fear of other men taking their lives or possessions? We can agree then that murder and theft are disliked by the majority of men, and these acts should merit consequences, should they not?

What about the condition of lying or false testimony about another? This has the potential to defame an individual, harming his character deeply. Others will lose trust in one, such as this based upon untruths told by another. Lying about another can have a snowball-on-a-hill effect, gathering more snow as it gains momentum.

Would it be safe to say then that men, by and large, would agree that lying about the life of another should have consequences? If the answer is yes, who would impose such consequences? Often men are not able to discern whether an individual is telling the truth or not. It can be extremely and painstakingly difficult to determine the truth of a matter.

Next is the act of coveting. What exactly does it mean to "covet" that which belongs to another (as *Webster* would define it.)?

Personally, I believe that to covet means to lay siege to that which is not yours, using your mind as the vehicle by which you will gain ownership. Defined in this manner, there are *few* who would disagree that this act is despicable. Man does not work long hours each day, after educating himself for years, to have another man become despicable and despondent over not being able to have what another owns. This is wrong. It breeds contempt, and contempt breeds murder and deceit. It usually ends badly for those who persist in covetousness. Their level of satisfaction with life in general diminishes because they are spending far too much time and energy, desiring that which others have.

Again, who can discern the covetous nature of men to control it? Who can characterize it individual by individual? Who can penalize this behavior in an effort to control it? Certainly, it is not man's job to do so, for it is inherent in all of man to covet what belongs to others.

What is the answer to this dilemma? Meditate on it for a few seconds. Now you are thinking like the Creator. How can man's innate character be controlled or monitored to bring about positive corrections in his behavior while still giving man the choice to do good or evil?

It is a daunting task at best. But it is being attempted daily by one who knows all of life's dilemmas.

At the moment, man is not awake enough to recognize his need for correction. All men live as though someone else is the enemy; when in fact, it is within us all to do evil. The battle to overcome this nature is won in the mind and then ultimately displayed by the change in the nature of men.

What is the answer to this flawed nature of men? Step by step, men must override thoughts of evil and temptation; for to give into this adversarial nature is to invite one who is purely evil and delights in those who do likewise. He must be avoided at all costs.

Later we will discuss the consequences of invoking an alliance with evil, for it will cost you more than your life in this body. You will pay with your eternal life.

CAPTIVE AUDIENCES

What exactly do I mean by "captive audiences"? I have chosen this phrase to represent mankind in his position to the enemy. He is a captive audience, so to speak. The enforcer of good in the world is able to manipulate man's will by simply speaking words after him. These words are then heard, considered, and most often acted upon by unsuspecting men, women, and children.

"How can this be happening without our knowledge?" you might ask. Again, it is simple. That which is speaking to man to influence his behavior is not of the flesh and blood sort. He possesses another nature. Some like to call that nature "spirit" or "demons" or the devil; but whatever way you look at it, they are not human.

If they are not human, how are we to separate ourselves from them? First and foremost, man must learn to stay clean, pure, and without evil. In some cultures, evil doings are identified by any deviation from an agreed-upon standard of living or code of conduct followed by the masses. It is reasonable to expect a people group to determine what behaviors are acceptable and unacceptable to most of the people, is it not?

It is not that difficult to surmise that some actions will be welcomed by communities and others will be rejected and, if evil, even punished. This establishes peace and harmony among men.

The trouble begins when a minority group rises up against the standard of living agreed upon by society and attempts to eradicate them for personal or evil reasons. The result can only be chaos, unless the majority maintains strength when under pressure from the nonconformists. There is no other way to keep peace in the land. We have perfect modern day examples of this today in nations where radical groups seek control over people and rise up to do evil against the established and accepted norm.

The answer lies in the people themselves. They must desire to see good perpetuated at all costs. They must maintain the majority rule that best serves the safety and goodness of the people. To do anything less is to risk the development of anarchy in the society where this evil governing hand emerges.

Why is it that men have become complacent in opposing evil? Is it because there is so much of it today? Or is it because men have done so little that there is so much of it? Is it too late now for action?

The truth is that without an uprising by people whose intentions are for good and not for evil, there is no future for any nation. Evil men will have their way against an inactive, restraining force for good.

Do you doubt me?

Need I remind you of the terrors of the past when people embraced the dogma of evil men and perpetuated this same evil against their own citizens and others?

The outcome is never good, and many are made to suffer unjustly.

What then are the answers for those of us in the world today, who are not content to sit back and give rise to the likes of a Hitler?

Action is the answer—for every action, there is a reaction. We must put forth the truth in love. Homosexuality is not good for the people. It breeds deviancy, hatred, and jealousy, for the outcome of this type of relationship can never rival that between a man and a woman. There is no planned destiny for this type of union. However, men and women who marry and have children can look forward to a historical destiny of the family line created in children, grandchildren, and even great grandchildren. These children will possess distinctive markers identifying them as children of particular parents.

What greater destiny can man possess than to leave a little of himself behind when he departs this earth?

It is unmatched by the possessions and other achievements one can acquire here.

This is just one of the lies being perpetuated on mankind. Wake up! We are not alone in the universe, and there are those who would see the end of us if possible.

WATCHER'S EYES

How often have you heard people describe a situation where they felt a presence? It happens to just about everyone. You are alone in a room, whether it is daylight or not; and just as you turn your head, something darts out of sight. You know it was there for you, "felt it" before you spotted a glimpse of it. What was it? Can you even describe it to another if you were to share the incident? Most likely, you will think twice before relating the details to someone, lest they think you have lost your mind. This does not negate your experience whatsoever, however, due to the fact that there are those who are spiritually connected and open-minded versus those who are not so.

You will find in this world those seeking the truth and those who are not. It may just be a matter of experiencing some downtime due to vacation or illness or such that allows your mind to process. Opportunities must present themselves in order for the mind to think creatively.

Once the mind and heart are open to embrace the supernatural, a person becomes more aware of its activity in our midst. There is good supernatural activity just as there is evil. The trick is gaining the experience necessary to diffuse what is good from what is evil.

"How does one do this?" you ask.

First things first.

Things must be in order, for there is one who follows a system of checks and balances; without that, you could lose your life investigating the truth. This is not some super hype included here to sell books. It is written for one purpose and one alone—to protect you and your life and even those of your loved ones from evil.

The supernatural world is difficult to comprehend at best. That which exists there operates on a different system than we do. Added to this fact is the dilemma that these who live beyond our sight have run amuck of their mission. They were created for the purpose of controlling the greater evil nature of men. As men would test the waters to see what they could "pull off," so to speak without consequences, this force—supernatural albeit force—would exact some kind of payment for the evil that men would do.

How does this compute for today? The truth is that the force is still in place; unfortunately, it has overridden its original program, and is now in fact perpetuating an evil of its own doing. This sounds frightening I know, but we not without a hope. There is a means to fight this force. It begins by serving the greater good of mankind. Choose to do the good that is within you, and you will not *often,* and I emphasize often, encounter his wrath.

The sadness of the situation is that "he," if we can assign gender, knows no boundaries anymore. "His" internal circuitry is malfunctioning. He is extracting from men, payment for their sins against a partially unwritten law that men are good. When men go against this internal law, the supernatural was to kick in to suppress the evil, redirecting men to do good rather than evil.

This system worked for some time until the supernatural enforcer of good lost his way, so to speak. He is on a crash course with extinction if man plays his cards right.

The essential ingredient to mankind's freedom is his awareness of the truth. This requires an awakening of sorts of his true nature. Man is not simply an organic body; in fact, he is so much more.

In the tenets of faith, this is most often described as eternal life. This has a measure of truth in it. There is life that exists beyond the body that is greater, more powerful, and without decay. Those people who go on from this world and who return to this existence experience jubilance and exultation. It is indescribable, for to attempt to describe what one has yet to experience is meaningless.

Experience is the measuring tool for all of life's endeavors. It is a tool used to train our minds in choosing good versus evil.

Why then is there such a great evil that exists in the world today? It is simple. That which was created as a balancing force in the world to control evil is now itself choosing to do evil. It is a paradox for sure.

Again, if this is true, what hope do we have in this world? Again, we must choose to do the good, which is within him to do. This is one way to protect one's self, and even in this system, there are flaws.

For instance, good men and women want to know why bad things "happen" to them. Again, this supernatural force knows no boundaries. His intentions are not for the good of man. He searches out those with an evil agenda, and then he supernaturally joins forces with them to fulfill their evil plans. This is *why* there is so much success in the world's evil and wicked men today. They are hidden from sight. They are protected by evil. They are given plans and schemes to bring about success. This is a worry for mankind.

On the other hand, man has access to his Creator. Like the Creator, we have great knowledge of evil and its ways, its agenda, and its strategies. We are able, as the Almighty, to counterbalance this evil with greater weapons and strategies. But in order to do so, we must have people who are *awake* and ready to listen. This is easier said than done. There are many reasons that mankind is "asleep." It is not all due to awareness or not of the supernatural. Some of this dullness of mind is due to unnatural food sources being consumed for food. These "foods" are not foods at all, but a dirty trick by evil to take the lives of men using the desire of men for money as the catalyst preservatives, pesticides, insecticides, hormones, and excess salt and sugar are all wrecking havoc with the body. A case in point is the rising cases of cancer and heart disease in the affluent nations of the world. Instead of using their monies to grow more natural, healthy goods, these nations are promulgating fast foods instead.

In order to have food that fast on a daily basis, shortcuts are taken, compromises are made to bring this "false" food to the table "fresh." Thus, greater and greater efforts are made to make "food" look fresh that if it were truly analyzed as such would not merit being called food at all.

What can we do to protect ourselves? The unfortunate news is that because of all that goes on against good health for the benefit of money, it is no easy task. Men must work hard to purge their bodies of impurities and then pursue a healthy means of eating if he is to see the greatest benefits of life in this body.

Where do we begin?

Fortunately, there is much truth available to us already. Organic farmers are contributing to better health. Vitamins and minerals are being sold that are essential to optimum health. Corrective measures can be taken to restore one's health and peace of mind. It is not too late to begin, but begin now! Add years to your life.

A SOLUTION

If mankind can live forever and for the sake of discussion in this book, let's assume that he does, then what is the purpose of the body? Why experience all of the pain, both emotional and physical, that accompanies life in these bodies? Surely, there is a good reason for the experience of life in an organic body that surpasses our understanding for many do question why man must suffer at all.

First, it is not as though man was meant to suffer. He was created to allow his forever spirit the experience of a body. This may sound too foreign or scientific for your taste, but it is true. The forever spirit is the one having the experience, and the body is the means to an end.

"What end?" you might ask.

As forever spirits, life is eternal. Continued opportunities arise to experience this life as a forever spirit. In the process of certain experiences, however, the forever spirits have been traumatized. You might equate this to the trauma suffered by men or women who return from war only to find loved ones gone, children dispersed, and the culture disrespectful or unresponsive to your needs. As a forever spirit, you are experiencing all things good and bad. It is your Creator's quest to remove the trauma from your forever spirits so that you may relish the good that you have experienced in the body and let go of the bad. In fact, it is essential to your healing as forever spirits.

Many are those who never heal. Their minds are filled with the horrors of life impacting their forever spirit negatively. For such, it is difficult to connect again with their forever or eternal nature apart from being healed first.

This is what your Creators are attempting to accomplish in the world today—the healing of mankind. It is a daunting task indeed due to the evil that is at work to defy us and impede our progress.

How then shall it be accomplished? It will be accomplished through the awakening of men's spirits to their true nature. A process in the minds of men must begin by which men let go of the body and embrace their minds. They must get control of their thoughts that ultimately impact their actions.

It takes time and dedication, but it must be accomplished. Men ought to be enjoying their encounters with organic bodies; but instead, there is much heartache, pain, and sorrow. This should not be so. It can be changed by an understanding of the mind. Man needs a mind encounter.

This is the solution that will bring understanding—an in-depth study of how the mind works and affects our lives must take place if men are to be free as forever spirits.

PLANS ABATED

The purpose of this chapter will be to identify for many of you how your specific goals and plans may be shifted by an understanding of how the mind works. Critical to the understanding of this, however, is that not all of our thoughts are our own. Thought is a cosmic quality in many respects. It exists in the universe. It can be embraced by humanity or rejected as such. This decision is made according to man's belief system.

One can entertain just about any conceivable religious system he could conceive of in this world. He can follow that school of thought to the letter, choosing to obey the tenets of that system by choice. It is not uncommon for individuals to do so, for a season of their lives only to later begin to listen to other presumptions of faith or truth. Does this now make the first school of thought defunct, or does it simply mean that mankind is free to choose the ideas for his own life?

I choose to believe the latter. Man has within him the freedom to choose what thoughts to entertain each day and what segments of society to interact with socially and corporately. This applies generally with most societies except for the totalitarian governments where freedom of choice is denied. In these societies, public opinion is constantly swayed by government intervention and indoctrination. Those under such a harsh system suffer the loss of freedom that comes from choosing which thoughts one wishes to indulge upon.

Having said these things, let us return to the discussion of thought. How much of what you hear every day is your own free thought? The truth is that most of us spend about 50 % of the time thinking about thoughts that are introduced to us throughout a given day. Think about it. Upon awakening, you turn on a radio or TV to hear the news or weather reports. You encounter your spouse or children who share their thoughts with you. As you start up your car, the radio again assaults you with the "truth." If you own and use cell phones, you are bombarded with messages from others about their needs with little or no regard for your own plans for the day.

This system requires that you care more for the others around you than you do for yourself. How does this come about? Each individual making demands of you to "care more" is projecting energy around you.

What is the source of this energy?

The energy we are talking about here is supernatural. It exists outside your plane of sight. It is powerful and negative in nature and controlling. Its desire is to make you care more, do more, give up more, cry more, experience pain more, and on and on. In fact, this concept gave rise to the word *karma* used in many cultures and religions sects. Karma simply means "kar-ma" or "care more".

What can be accomplished when man cares more about others than himself? Well, generally very little unless the person receives your help and assistance. We have all encountered people who reject the help of others. What happens in the minds of those who reject the help of others? Two possibilities come immediately to mind. The person offered help who rejects it must then reconcile his own dilemma without the assistance of others. Secondly, those who offered the help in the first place may take it upon themselves to "fix" the person. This sets up a third scenario that involves the supernatural. There is an energetic field that surrounds each individual. When a person cares more than is necessary or received on the other side, the person in pain sends off negativity toward the person wanting to help him. This can cause great anguish to those caregivers in this world. You see, not everyone wants our help or needs it.

"How can this be?" you say.

For years, we have learned to love others as we love ourselves. Doesn't this include bringing about change in the lives of others too? The answer is an emphatic no. Each person is having his own experience of life within boundaries set by himself and to some extent *fate*. As a computer has data imprinted into it, so does man. It is in the DNA. It is a form of pre-destiny. DNA determines sex, blood type, bone structure, predestination toward certain diseases, etc.

Man's destination is inherent from birth, or is it? Is it possible to break out of the mold and reject the predestination code written for you? The answer to this question is a resounding yes. But know this it will be a battle within yourself to do so.

Does this mean one should not attempt it? On the contrary, it is a challenge to do so. It is evolving into your greater potential. It is not only possible, but invigorating and exulting.

It is the way to freedom.

IMPOSSIBLE DREAM

There is a hope that lies within each one of us that we will live life to the fullest exampled by wealth, love, a legacy of children, and generosity to others. Unfortunately, this is nothing more than the impossible dream to millions of men and women in the world who suffer their particular plight in life. The admonition to them from the world's religious is to enjoy their lives as best they can, for God gives as He will to men. This is a nice story but has little truth in fact.

Men who seek to rise above their circumstances in life often do so to the surprise of many. Success stories are a dime a dozen of the poor, the uneducated, the underprivileged, and even the chronically sick overcoming bleak circumstances only to find joy and success in the world.

Does this defy your logic? Let me give you a few examples. Sammy Souza, born poor, but despite the odds, rose to be one of the most recognized band and march leaders of all time. Einstein was not wealthy nor was Ben Franklin; however, they were gifted. They chose to pursue their gifts rather than money. In this was the greater joy.

The world is a difficult place. Men do not rise to their destinies without a struggle. Even in those families where money is a given, you will find that men and women had to work hard on their own effort to achieve success. Rarely in this world do we find those who simply sit on their empires without lifting a finger. There is work to be done even by the wealthy to run a corporation if it is to be successful. How many of you really want to work hard? The answer is again few.

Few and far between are those willing to go the distance to be all they can be. Do you doubt this statement? Take your own survey of your friends. How many would be willing to work sixty-hour weeks for a year for a million dollars. Ask them. I assure you that your list will not be as long as you think.

On the other hand, many will work hard to fulfill their destinies. It is an innate desire. Their days are filled with thoughts of fulfilling the impossible dream.

These individuals are willing to pay the price climbing every mountain, overcoming every obstacle, and paying any price. These people are our true heroes, for fate comes to all of mankind. The issue here is how many will overcome fate to dream the impossible dream.

Are you one of them? What are you willing to do to acquire your dream? Will you go to school educating yourself in preparation? Will you miss a vacation or two to finish the task? What is most important to you? Follow the examples of the ones who have made it.

Dream the impossible dream.

HOPE RESTORED

Are you living right now in an absence of hope? Are you languishing away the days waiting for your "ship to come in" to solve all of your life's problems? My response to this is to stop waiting, get up, and do something. Time waits for no one as they say. Those who are 100 percent actively pursuing their destinies are some of the most satisfied individuals on the planet. They set goals and set things in motion to achieve those goals.

Few and far between are those who, upon leaving this earth, say, "I've done all that I wanted to do, and I'm ready to go." Man always has regrets. "If only I had done this or that" is a common phrase heard by the dying. If only I had loved more, worked harder, saved more money, taken more vacations, and on and on.

The list of regrets is endless for those who neglected to pursue their dreams. If you at least spend a portion of time pursuing your dream, you can find peace at the end of your days.

So what are you waiting for? Go for it!

The essence of all hope is the personal knowledge of a better outcome if certain parameters of life are adhered to along the way. We make decisions early on in life based upon a plan for ourselves for the future. We determine from weighing the experiences of others what might best work for us to get us an A or B if we can simply follow a certain course of action. This may or may not include higher education, job experience, and personal relationships. We set our minds on a particular goal and begin to work toward achieving that goal. The outcome of such an endeavor is tied to the desire we have to achieve our goals. How badly do we desire success, notoriety, wealth, and prestige? This is the gauge by which men will determine their success. How badly do they want it? We all know men who have set their minds on evil and achieved their goals. Why do we not ask men to set their intentions on the good that is within them to do? What about educating today's youth with the mindset that nothing is impossible unless you yourself say that it is impossible thereby imposing your own roadblocks to your own success.

What man needs is a little motivation. Are the parents of today's youth stimulating their children to go for the gold? Do we believe in our youth? What would your children say about you if asked if you were the inspiration for their lives? Do you emulate values that others uphold as worthwhile? Or are you only as good as you need to be and then only as others are "watching"? What happens when you think no one is watching? This is typical when your children are watching and listening intently to determine who you really are in their estimation. You make your greatest impressions when you are just simply being yourself. These are the memorable moments to your children.

They are looking for *you* to "be real." If they can actually capture you being real, you have made one of the greatest impressions on them of their lives. They will respect you more, love you for your transparency, and perhaps even generate a following. People today do not need a "perfect" role model to dictate terms of their behavior as much as they need to see "real" men and women facing real-life decisions—sometimes extremely difficult ones—but who choose to handle life's difficulties by drawing on a core set of values that help them determine a right response versus a wrong response.

This is best learned by experience; thus, it is wrong to judge another's life based upon your experience, for each man or woman must live his life experientially to determine the better way to handle what comes his way.

No two lives are exactly alike causing a different reality for each one of us. One cannot really know what it is like to experience life in another person's body. Each body has its own responses and emotions based on circumstances and relationships of the past. We can only examine life independently, sharing our experiences with others in the hopes that some of what we have learned may benefit another.

Again, life is best lived experientially day by day. When we plan ahead what we are going to do or say in many situations, we eliminate spontaneity and set our minds to go in one direction even when there may be a better possibility that comes to us in the moment. I am not talking about throwing away the planning for an education or wedding or career. I am speaking specifically about experiences. Let them happen and enjoy them, allowing yourself the freedom to choose what to say or do freely, not based upon what others have done or said or experienced. Follow your intuitive sense of goodness, and just do the right thing. It will work out fine.

BRIDGES CROSSED

There are bridges to cross over in life where underneath lies all of life's difficulties, heartbreaks, uncertainties, and painful memories. The idea is to get to the other side, escaping the running waters that would otherwise engulf you or *worse,* drown you.

Does everyone encounter these bridges? Indeed and often, it is far worse for others than it can be for you. Does this mean that we are somehow better than others if we escape life's greater tragedies? No, certainly not, but it may mean that we have approached the crossing with a little different mind-set than others have done.

How we look at life and the solemn tragedies of it will determine how healthy we are for the long haul. There is only one legitimate way through this life, and it is by experience.

Experience shapes our lives in numerous ways, some good and some bad. In particular, we would want to choose those experiences that would alter our lives only for good, but then where would the lessons of life come from by which we learn to make better choices?

Men are shaped by destiny certainly, but there is no denial by those who have experienced life that it is through the choices we are making that we uncover the truth that there is often a better way. Does it cost us something to choose the better way? Yes, often it does. We may have to invest more time, money, or ego to reach our goals, the better albeit harder way. But in the end the results are worth it. We can achieve our goals while choosing the path of least resistance, or we can achieve the same results by overcoming obstacles in a legitimate way where no one gets hurt. Which way do you think most people choose to go? You would be surprised how many people live to regret their life choices.

If you doubt this statement, simply ask around you if they regret any life choices that they have made. You will be surprised at their answers.

The simple truth is that all of us have hurdles to cross in life, but how we do it is what shapes us as individuals.

THE MARCH OF TIME

The march of time . . . what is it? Why is it? What does time mean, and why do we work to keep track of it? Are we deluded to think that time will end, and a new millennium will begin at some point, or are we living each day for the joy of it as we ought to be doing instead? There are a number of schools of thought out there on this subject right now, and some are looking for the end to come at any minute. This is unfortunate, for to do so is to live in fear rather than in hope of what each day can bring to your life. If we focus on the end rather than on the moment, we are not doing even what is recommended that we do in the Bible, which is to live each day for what it has to offer, for tomorrow has enough trouble of its own. I personally like this thought. Each day does have enough concern of its own, and to worry about what may or may not happen on the next day is just to preoccupy ourselves with the future instead of the present moment.

I believe that time will reveal itself to us as we live in this world, and we need not worry about it or focus on it with too much of our energy for life. Rather it might be a good idea to take the energy that we have to strive toward excellence in that which we desire to do with our lives in the body. Certainly, there is much to think about for the moment about our endeavors, families, health, entertainment, and purpose without further complicating the matter worrying about tomorrow. In fact, many are those who have saved for the future only to find that for them the future never came. They put all their money aside rather than to have spent it on themselves and their children enjoying life and were then robbed of the opportunity to enjoy it when ill health came along and preempted their plan. What good is a pile of money in old age if you don't make it to old age? It is prudent, yes, to plan for the future when you may not be working, but isn't it wise also to enjoy your life while you have your vitality and health? I have mixed emotions about putting all your extra monies in a bank or mutual funds or whatever while the good times pass you by. What are you going to do when you are old and gray? Sit around and count your money?

Enjoy your children and your grandchildren, and perhaps while doing so, they will appreciate you enough to help you when you need it should it become necessary to do so. Or are we too skeptical of human nature to trust that our own would be so kind and generous, and we have been to them? I hope not!

The passage of time is an inescapable part of life. It happens to everybody. Those who are most successful with time are those who will say that they accomplished everything that they wanted to do during the time that they were given on this earth. Those who did not use time wisely enough will have regrets unless they specifically deal with them ahead of time so that they can have peace when their time is up, so to speak. Is it possible to have lived only a portion of your dreams and plans and still find peace at the end of life? I believe so. Sometimes we awaken too late to what it is that we want to do, but it may be that not having done it is still okay. We can have enough of a good life in loving our families and friends, and what we did in this world to let go of it when it is the end of time for us. We must look at life as an experience and a journey. Whatever we take with us when we leave is now part of us eternally to relive and relish. All of the joys and pains of a life's experiences make up the existence in this world, and it is what it is.

We must examine what has happened to us here and accept it as part of our experience, letting go of the more painful experiences while embracing the wonderful experiences of life. Yet there is much to be learned from even the painful experiences of life. Sometimes we learn ourselves to be better people by having had an encounter with evil. Whatever our experiences here, they can bring about good if we let them.

If men are intent on doing evil, they will influence the lives of others in a strongly negative way. This will affect at least two people's lives with negative energy. How does one get rid of that negative energy forced upon their lives? It is a process, but it can be accomplished with love that reaches beyond anger, resentment, bitterness, hatred, sadness, and pain. It is a love that embraces all of life's experiences as part of the world experience. It is temporary. Life extends far beyond the body at the end of time for each of us. Our experiences will tell us much about humanity and his progress in life. We can help others more from eternity, knowing what it is like to live in the body and to suffer and to hurt. We hopefully will have learned how to love unconditionally, which can only be learned through experiences some more extreme than others. Mankind does not naturally love others. It is not a given. Mankind, in fact, looks for all the reasons *not* to love others. Why should we? They do this and that to us to harm us. They hurt us, shame us, and ridicule us. Why in the world should we just love them unconditionally? Who in their right mind does that? We have to have a reason after all, don't we? At least, that is the way that we think.

It is rare to find an individual that loves outside of himself for the sole purpose of giving love to another. Usually men want something in return for the love that they give. Why is that? It is in our nature to be so. We cannot change it by ourselves, but often times it is through experience that we see things differently and are able to love more unconditionally.

For instance, for men and women who become parents, there is an opportunity to love unconditionally and yet many still do not. They do not find it in their hearts to simply love this child that they have jointly created, but they set expectations even for this new creation before it is born. They will expect it to do this and that by a certain age, and if it does not, well there will be consequences and those consequences will usually be bad. Why is it that we cannot just love the child and let it experience life for itself? There is a reason here, isn't there? A child cannot comprehend the nature of the choices they are making. If they choose wrongly without knowing what may happen in a situation, it may cost them their lives. They must have a mentor over them who, out of love, desires to assist them in the making of their choices. While assisting them is great, every parent has learned that it is only through having negative consequences that we learned to make the better choice.

Do you now get a picture of how it is with our Creator? If there were no negative experiences in life, how is it that we would learn to make better choices? How is it that we would learn the experience of how to love? We needed to learn because it was not natural for us to do so. We questioned everything. Now many people are unable to accept that life is for this purpose. Once again, it will be by experience that they learn, otherwise and perhaps, they will never realize the deeper meaning of life. Hopefully, that will not be the case; for in the end, it is most important to recognize that life was a journey, and in that life was the good and the bad.

Now it is time for all of us to embrace the life that we have in the body and to live it to the fullest doing the good that is within us to do putting aside that which is evil. It is no longer a question of what is good and what is evil. Man has seen with his own eyes in this world that there is evil, and it is apparent everywhere. What will man do with this information? Will he choose to do good, or will he choose evil? Has he learned the lesson of which is better? What if God were to withdraw his hand for a season to test man's ability to live as he ought to live? How would we fair? Would we fail or would we persevere knowing that good is the better choice for humanity? I fear that there are a fair number of people in this world who have not learned the lesson for good yet. We are not ready as a people to be left to our own devices to figure out how to perpetuate good in the world.

We are still making many mistakes, and many people are still getting hurt because of it.

What then is the answer for humanity? A popular saying over the past few years has been, what would Jesus do? A better question is, what would men do if they had the chance to rule without a greater power in the universe looking after them? What would they do? What could we expect if men were ruling the planet uninhibited? I think that we can all answer that it would be a mess for sure. Without the restraining force in the world that appears to bring about an action against those who do evil, we would certainly experience chaos, would we not? In fact, we are already experiencing chaos in the world.

Why is that? Could it be that the restraining force once used to keep good men from doing evil has itself begun to do evil too? Is it possible that we do not know everything that there is to know about this world, and that there is such a force upon it working alongside evil men to cause harm to those of us who want to do good? I tell you the truth, such a force exists. What is the remedy for men to overcome such evil? Men must relent of doing evil and purpose in their hearts to do good, or all of men will be touched by this evil. It will be inescapable. We are already seeing damage being done to our lives by these forces of evil. New York paid a dear price for all of us in this nation. We must turn things around if we are to survive as people. Mankind must awaken to his real mission in life and begin to stand against the evil that surrounds them. If we continue on our present course of accepting all things as good, we will experience greater tragedy in the world as evil will do its job of balancing the universe, and even a bit more than what is its job of acting alongside those who do evil for success.

Does this sound too outlandish for words? I assure you that it is the truth. It is inspired truth, and it is upon you today to act upon it. Generations to come will be affected by this truth; in fact, they already are being affected by it. We are seeing the results of what is happening when the truth is not taught to schoolchildren, and when they are told that all things are acceptable in society. Evil begins to work to balance the situation. Harm comes to those institutions by way of evil. There is no way to stop it for it is powerful to work alongside of man for success when it sees an imbalance in the world. It is doing its job, so to speak, whether we like it or not. We can correct it only by doing what is good for ourselves and our children. Teaching anything less will bring harm to them and directly to us for they are loved by us.

We are in a sad state of affairs in this nation. We are mocked around the world and called names inappropriately for what we have become known for in the United States. What is it that is so upsetting to other cultures? What is it that they fear that we would bring to their nations if we were to integrate with them there? Is it perhaps that they do not want to bring a drug culture to their nations? Is it that public sex and nudity is not wanted in every culture around the world? Perhaps they do not want their children exposed to sex, lies, and videotapes. Is it any wonder when we have the greatest number of teens having sex in the world? Alongside of that, we have a highly inappropriate number of abortions to accompany that statistic. Children are aborting their children while the school systems are being set up to assist them in doing so without the approval of the parents. What are we doing? How can we call this good for the nation or its people?

We cannot, and we will suffer for it. There will be a price extracted for this kind of teaching of our people and our children. We will pay a price in lives taken by the one who is trained to do so when evil is perpetuated in a society. He knows how to do it, and he enjoys his work.

Am I attempting to put fear into the hearts of the people? The answer is a resounding no. I am attempting to put goodness back into the hearts of the people. I am asking people to awaken to their true purpose for being in the body, which is to enjoy and love life and people. We are not here to run amuck of every good and perfect thing, only to do the sick and twisted thing instead. We are not here to become perverted with our children or ourselves, but to love one another and to be a blessing to one another's lives with the good that we can do here. What will happen if we continue on the path that we are choosing to do evil rather than good? Only our Creator can answer that one, but I can assure you, it will not be pretty.

Knowing this, we must assist one another in reawakening to a greater life purpose, and turn this nation around for good. Is this too daunting a task for us? It better not be, for the consequences of doing nothing will be more tragedy for us and for the generations to come.

Rise up, people, and take back the land! Stand for truth and righteousness. This is not a religious fanatic's cry, but rather it is the cry of the love of goodness rising up in the land. Decency and purity must again be taught in our schools along with kindness and love. Children have no need of learning about sexuality in school. Believe me, they are getting plenty education on the subject with their peers, and hasn't that always been the case? We must return to the basics and teach our children well, how to grow into good, decent human beings, reaching for the stars in pursuing their own success in the world. Then the blessings will come to them, to us, and to our nation. I relent.

A TIME TO LIVE

There is a time to live and time to die. This we know to be true, but right now for millions of people on this planet, it is a time to live. Unfortunately without a bit of education, many people will not live, they will die.

"Why is that?" you ask.

They will die due to the lack of knowledge of how to live. Living requires the knowledge of a number of things. First, of course, is the knowledge of nutrition. What are the basic tenements of good health? Perhaps I should list them here. They are nutritious food, clean available water, and protection from the elements. Now is a good time to review with you what I mean by "the elements." In particular, I am speaking of heat, cold, rain, and ice.

However, in addition to these four, there are numerous other elements of the world endangering us. They are such as arachnoids, reptiles, and insects. Even farther down the food chain are the microscopic organisms threatening mankind. These are microbiological in nature. They are spores of molds, mildew, virus, and influenza. These microscopic organisms can wreck havoc on man's ability to breathe normally. Once this is accomplished and the immune system is hindered, these microorganisms establish themselves quite nicely within the human body its self, thriving in its dark moist internal environment.

Mankind is just now gaining the advantage over some of these biological enemies of man. But there is much more to learn, and time really is of the essence in many cases. Abundant storms of rain and snow have brought much moisture to parts of the United States, not familiar with how to deal with it.

Molds and mildews will run rampant without a remedy. Adding to this new dilemma is the inconsistency of men to always do the right thing. Molds are microscopic and need very little of an opening to gain entrance to your home. The spores of black molds are insidious in nature. They are viable under the most extreme climate conditions. They do not need a sustained stream of moisture to survive but in fact can exist where a minimum of moisture can be provided even intermittently.

What then shall be our defense? We must see that our homes are built as though they were a living, breathing organism, for in many ways they are just that—alive.

Think about it. By its very nature, most homes are organic. Homes built close to the ground often with very little separating them from the ground. The ground itself is teeming with microorganisms. These microorganisms can gain access to the inside of your home through the tiniest concrete cracks, and don't believe those who, for money's sake, will tell you otherwise. The dangers are real once these microorganisms gain *access* to your home.

"Why?" you ask.

Because your home provides more nutrition for them than they had before the home was built. Specifically, molds can feed off plaster residue, paint chips, wool and other organic carpeting, human flab of skin and nails, and the list goes on. As mentioned before, their existence does not require an abundance of water. The night air in many instances is sufficient enough for mold to live.

Crawl spaces and basements provided the much-needed aeration for purposes of containing moisture at the base of a home. Unfortunately, adding a basement or crawl space adds expense and time to any project, thereby jeopardizing the viability of some housing projects.

By the time the problem of mold and mildew reveal themselves, many developers are long gone spending their money, warranties have expired, and the homeowner must now reconcile his own house problems while perhaps remaining thousands even millions of dollars in debt.

This leaves an imbalance in the universe. One person or group reaps the benefits of cheaper construction while leaving another to not only suffer serious health issues but financial consequences as well.

In the universe, all things must be balanced. Our Creator will see to it, you can be sure.

Every action brings a reaction.

Those who perpetuate such harm against others will pay a price, and it will be carried out by the one who sees all and knows all.

IMPROMPTU WISDOM

What is the source of all knowledge in your mind? Where does knowledge come from? Does it originate in your mind or are you "programmed with a certain degree of intelligence"? Could it be that there is a superior intelligence in the universe that proportions knowledge and wisdom to men in accordance with their current understanding and ability to grasp new knowledge? I prefer to believe the latter.

We are limited as humans as to what new thoughts we can originate; however, we can receive and analyze new data just as a computer can be upgraded and updated. Is this too simpleminded for you? I assure you that it is true; if it were not, what is the purpose of higher education if we are not capable of embracing new thoughts that originate from outside of *ourselves*?

We are uniquely constructed to be programmable with new insights and mindsets. This has been shown to be dangerous knowledge in the hands of certain elite groups who master its probabilities. Could it be that we are already experiencing a cultural mind control by those in our media not to mention universities and undergraduate schools? Are our youth being steered to "think" a certain way as a means to controlling a nation? Is goodness being promoted or extricated as intolerant of others' choices?

Men and women with an agenda to form lifetime opinions about faith, national pride, and prejudice are inculcated into our schools everywhere. They are against the norm that made

America free and strong. They are generally anti-faith due to its freeing nature. Men and women of faith tend to awaken to the truth that they need only follow the dictates of their own hearts to choose to do good and much joy can belong to them.

This is a threat to the controlling elite. They must not allow it. It has taken much time and money on their part to position their following in power throughout the country. They hide behind ideals of democracy, but indeed their agenda is quite insidious. Rob the people of their freedom to choose by eliminating their choices by intimidation and talk of tolerance. What man stands a chance to have more than two children if everyone he knows says that it is selfish to use so much of the earth's resources for his own family heritage. How dare he? Who does he think that he is after all? The pope?

This controlling mentality is prevalent in our midst, and yet we do not acknowledge it as "controlling" but rather as liberal minded.

All mankind has the right to choose for his self what manner of life he will pursue. Whether it is to be married, unmarried, educated or uneducated, simple life or more complex, rich or poor, it really is a matter of choice. Many are those who have risen from adversity only to go on to higher education and success through nothing more than sheer determination to do so. Who can fault these people for achieving their success? Should they be made to feel badly for their success?

What kind of individual robs the joy of another such as this? The jealous person, an evil person, a dissatisfied and disingenuous person, that's who.

The *day* will come when these people are exposed for their true nature, and it is in the not-too-distant future.

Pray for it.

Ask for it.

Expose them for who they are, and soon those whose intentions are for good and not for evil will rise to the top as they should.

I repose.

ADEQUATE FORUM FOR TRUTH

What is an adequate forum for truth? Let us coin a phrase here today and establish its meaning for others to embrace. An adequate forum for truth is one that is open to all schools of thought, but which *allows* the individual to choose the belief system that is best suited to his way of thinking. An adequate forum does not seek to steer thought in any one particular direction, thus eliminating free choice and intellect to function, but rather it presents all sides, without any intent to shape the minds of those listening. You share your opinion, and if it deviates from my own, then I will relate my opinion. Let your own intellect decide who is correct. How does that sound? Does it sound more like a free society than one where a college professor intimidates students to write a particular paper, idealizing particular thoughts that are not his own with the threat of a punitive action or grade if he or she does otherwise?

Which way appeals to you to learn? Learning should be the process of taking in new thoughts and ideas and then forming an intelligent analysis of what you have learned based on facts, not hearsay or opinion.

When we can achieve this free expression in teaching and learning, society will have matured so as not to be threatened by those who choose their own opinions. It is greatly needed if we are to be truly free.

Mankind was not created to be a pawn for one particular group's ideals, but rather to seek personal fulfillment based upon his inward search for truth. In the pursuit of truth is the discovery of the better path of goodness. It benefits all of humanity, but each man must come to his own deeper understanding of this truth.

COGNITIVE FREEDOM

What exactly does cognitive freedom means? There is a state of being free that must be felt to be properly experienced. It cannot simply be defined by one or another, but it must be experienced to the fullest in order to be understood. I myself have experienced this state of freedom. What exactly am I experiencing freedom from, you might ask. I am experiencing a freedom from the mindset that I must follow a preset order of rules or laws set by men, or I am not free. I disagree with this position on freedom. I am not required to follow the rules of men or tenets of their faith system in order to be free. I am free merely because I choose to be free from the evil that is in the world and to do his will rather than to do the good that is in me. I choose freely to do good rather than evil. This is the freedom that all men have on this earth. If every man would choose to do good rather than evil, the world would be a much more desirable place, would it not?

Mankind has longed to comprehend the way to freedom, but it is really not all that difficult to grasp. In order to be free, man must choose good rather than evil. In the course of mankind, men have often chosen the latter rather than the former, and the results are evident throughout history. Fallen civilizations were the norm for the past record. Why is this? This is the decline of man who seems to prefer to entertain evil than to continue to do that which is proven to be the better and safer way to go. What is in the nature of man that pushes him to do evil rather than to pursue a life of pure goodness and to prosper from doing so? Why does man do what will only to bring him trouble? It is in his nature to do so. He is "programmed" per se to test the waters so to speak.

This is how men learn to choose good rather than evil. Evil has attached to it certain outcomes and consequences when practiced in a society that has established norms of behavior. Men do not have to follow the established patterns of behavior acceptable to the greater population, but if they choose not to do so, there are certain consequences to them for choosing otherwise. Man cannot learn otherwise, for the experiential nature of man is inherent in him and has been since the beginning of time. He must "test the waters" to see what works best. Much has been accomplished through this process of learning. "Why?" you say. Because men also have a nature of not giving up until they accomplish what it is that they are attempting to do. This process of learning right from wrong is essential to the greater development of the mind in every individual. It is the way to growth and stimulates intellectual ability. Every parent can cite examples to this one. Children learn best by experiencing their choices and the ramifications of them. A parent can tell a child what will happen if they do such and such, but the child is not likely to choose not to do a thing until he experiences the negative consequences of doing it for himself. It does not mean that a parent is negligent or inept when their child chooses to do something against their will or advice and suffers consequences. The choice remains with the one making it. He will feel responsible for the outcome of his own choices, and this will shape and form his life and future choices. This is how it is supposed to be.

We are interested in the experiences of others to a point, but then it is time for us to venture out and do the thing that we are inclined to do just to see whether we can do it or not. If it ends badly, then that is the reality that we are faced with for the choices we have chosen, is it not? It is no one else's fault, and no one else need accept responsibility or blame for another's choices. We each are responsible for the things that we choose to do in this world. Too much assigning of blame has taken place in the world today, and young people are not required to be responsible for their actions. It is always someone else's fault that a thing occurred and not their own. How convenient. This does not teach a person anything useful, but in fact, it weakens their resolve to learn from their mistakes and to grow up. Consequences for our actions serve as a great teacher to shape our futures. We must allow them to occur if we are to continue to see minds being properly guided for success. It is the best way and has been proven to work very nicely. Our actions bring a reaction in this universe either good or bad. We have to decide from the outcome of our actions which reaction we prefer and then seek it. Chances are the majority would prefer a good outcome to a negative one, and the world will be a better place.

The danger lies in parents or others in positions of authority not allowing the natural consequences to occur for deviant behavior, but rather they justify improper behavior due to extenuating circumstances that may have lead to the individual choosing to do bad rather than good. This is simply a manipulation to avoid the obvious consequences due those who choose to do evil. This is nothing more than trickery by those who know how to do it. It leads to chaos in the society when those who do evil go unpunished for their deeds against others. Therefore, what is the solution?

Mankind must return to the simple explanation of what is good and what is evil. "What is that?" you say. Good question. Good is that which benefits yourself or others in such a way to bring no harm to yourself or anyone else in acquiring the good that you desire. Let's look at an example. Suppose that you are interested in achieving higher education. This is a good thing to do. It is acceptable to the society around you that you would do so, and you can receive assistance in some instances to accomplish this good for yourself. Oftentimes, scholarships are available, and government loans—banks will often assist you with loans, or family and friends if they are able to do so. It is a rare thing to find someone who would object to you doing this good for yourself.

On the other hand, should you decide to get drunk and get behind the wheel of a car, this is not a healthy thing to do for yourself or for the others that are using the same road systems that you are at anytime. This is not a good choice for anyone to make, and should something happen and you should harm yourself or another in the process of driving your vehicle while intoxicated, there should be a minimum of consequences to you for having done such a thing. The problem is that in this society today, people are making lame excuses for the behaviors that they do that bring about harm to others. They blame parents, school officials or teachers, employers, the words of others but refuse to accept responsibility for their own actions. How has this happened today? Is it because parents do not want to see their children suffer? Is it because we have seen too much suffering in the world and no longer want to see any more of it regardless of whether the individual deserves it for his own actions caused harm to himself or others? It is ludicrous to assume this way of thinking.

Chaos will ensue in the society when there are no consequences for evil actions against humanity.

Mankind is already seeing the degeneration of its society due to the improper handling of evil men. If the society does not get a handle on this backward thinking, it will surely suffer greatly in the generations to come. Evil must be punished if civil society will survive.

THE RISE AND FALL OF FAITH

What is behind the rise and fall of the faith? What is the purpose of faith, i.e., belief in a higher power, and how can it define our days on earth while continuing to liberate us?

Is there some unique quality to the liberty found through Christ's example that isn't found elsewhere? If so, what is it? Is it available to all men? Remember when I use the word *men* I refer more broadly to mankind that is inclusive of all women.

According to the scriptures, "Faith is the substance of things hoped for, the evidence of things not seen." Please note that this passage is found in Hebrews 11:1. You may refer to http:// bible.cc/hebrews/ll-1.htm. This is a very true statement. Faith or belief in a higher power and in the forgiveness of our sins has a liberating tenet in it. If we can be forgiven for our sins, then we need not fear death, correct? If this is true for all men not just some, how much more liberating is this truth to the many "marked" men who sit in our prisons having done harm to others? This premise of truth is unprecedented in the world today.

Man's existence in the world then is not to suffer for the wrong they have done according to faith but rather to learn from his mistakes such that he can move on at the end of his days. Is this world the only experience each of us will have in life? I don't believe so. I believe we will encounter many more realities once this one has passed, but we will do it by choice.

I cannot offer you proof certain at this juncture; however, I have had encounters with the spirits of those who have departed this earth. These were not negative experiences at all but rather were given to me as a measure of truth of the afterlife for myself and those who might also believe.

The messages I received were encouraging, enlightening, and filled with love for me and others. They provided comfort and peace to those whose hearts were grieving at the loss of a loved one.

There are those of the faith who do not believe in such things. The truth is that we seldom do believe in that which we do not experience for ourselves. The revelation comes to us in the experience itself; hence, we are so enlightened and made believers.

I can say unequivocally that I am a believer, not because of someone else's persuasion or talk about matters of faith. I have encountered the supernatural face-to-face, and this made a believer out of me. Thus, it should be so for every man, for that which we personally experience cannot be denied. Correct? Who can discount the truth of something they did not experience? It is your word against their own, and it doesn't matter ultimately, for each man must have his own experience with life in order to speak of it from the heart.

I have had experiences of the supernatural that could have driven me to despair, but in fact, these situations have merely made me stronger and ultimately more free. What is absolutely imperative to encountering pure, unadulterated truth is a pure mind; without which, you are merely viewing a situation through the programmed response of another.

Learning how to have your own unique experience of life will bring you the greatest joy. Instead of reading five to six books on a subject prior to experiencing it for yourselves, why not just jump in? See what the experience will bring. Set aside the fear and move out. It is liberating to do so.

Mark your days by the new experiences you allow yourself to embrace, learning new things being moved by nature's beauty firsthand, marking time by the joy you have with life through your experiences. This having been said, "Enjoy!"

The greatest message ever given in this world was "love as I have loved you." In the giving of love, your experience on earth will be more greatly enhanced and rewarding, but never should it be done at the expense of self.

It is crucial to grasp this concept. One must maintain the self in order to continue to draw from what he has to give another.

THE CONCLUSION OF THE MATTER

If man is not alone, and there is an evil force within the earth that is interacting with man against his will and his knowledge, what is man to do to combat this interference from the supernatural? It is not an easy matter but can be done through a combination of factors. One is that man must first understand that he is mind, body, and soul. His mind can and does interact with the spiritual aspects of this world. The important thing to remember is that there is a good and evil side to the spiritual realm. Man must learn how to recognize the evil spiritual influence in order to gain the advantage over it. This is difficult if men continue to blur the differences between good and evil. While men may "forget" how to do good, the force in the world that is watching will not forget. He will continue to exact payment for every wrong done by men until man either wakes up and follows the path to goodness or loses the battle.

It is essential at this point to remind you that man is to participate with his Creator in maintaining his good health. There is a good way to eat and a bad way to eat. One will support the body and its systems, and the other will be sure to cause you an early death or at the very least sickness and ill health. It is not the desire of your Creator to see you suffer in any way due to the bodies malfunctioning; however, much of what is causing man's sicknesses is due to the inappropriate diets and lifestyles of man himself. It can hardly be blamed on the Creator when a man chooses to live on nothing but hotdogs and buns without including any vegetables or fruits or supplements to increase the health of the body in this vitamin-depleted world.

Next is the notion that man is only a body and not spirit. This is simply not true. All men were created as spirit first and given a body later as part of a spiritual exercise in eternity. It can only be best understood by acknowledging a bit of faith in the matter. We cannot possibly understand it all due to the very fact that we have not experienced it yet in our minds. It is "hidden" from us in a sense so that we are focused on the experience that we are having at the moment. How would it be if man were to spend his every waking moment longing for the reality of the place he left rather than enjoying the reality that he is experiencing at the moment? What fun would that be? There is great fun and experience to be had by men if they would only participate in the world in a good way, ignoring the evil and not embracing it but rather fighting for the good that is within him to do in this world. The world would be a better place. It can still happen if men will awaken to their truer destinies and move ahead.

THE FINAL CONCLUSION

In summarizing the notions brought forth in this book, I must begin with this truth. All truth is relative to those who *believe* it. In other words, for those who are not yet ready to embrace the truth of this book, they quite simply will *not* do so. On the other hand, there are those spread throughout the world at large that are more than ready to understand their predicament here on this earth. They are ready to embrace the tenets of this truth and to experience it in all its splendorous freedom. It is to these individuals that I write this book. It is my desire that hearts would be opened to knowing that the end is not near if men are willing to stand for something good in this world and to work toward establishing it.

The work of establishing freedom must be done by all men eventually in order to see that it is established for the greater good. If not, then those who would work against freedom will have the upper hand. We all know that in order for evil to rise up, good men need only sit back and do nothing and it will be accomplished. It is the nature of the order of things in this world. We have seen it before, and we will see it again if something does not rapidly change the status quo. Men must embrace the truth that evil choices bring about consequences to those who do evil and to those who allow it. If mankind is not willing to take the necessary steps to curtail the uprising of evil, then mankind will fail. It is as simple as that.

What will be the greater destiny of men will be determined by the whole, not just a few. When men make up their minds to allow those who lead a less moral lifestyle to control the masses, there is a price to be paid, and usually it becomes recognizable in the upcoming generations that follow such outlandish behaviors as those of the homosexual community. It is inevitable that the society must pay for the promotion of immorality.

The long-term effects of such behavior will be felt by the nations that serve such deviant behaviors and those who practice them. A better choice for the nations would be to embrace the lifestyles that promote harmony in the culture. Rewriting the script of what makes a good marriage does not have a worthy intention for the future of nations. It can only bring about disharmony for the lost children of broken relationships and wayward thinking about the natural intended unions designed for men and women and for the destiny of the family lines. Without two partners cohabitating in marriage as man and wife, there would be no future generations. Granted children are born out of wedlock as a regular course, but their family destiny is lost in the process often if for no other reason than that the child is swept off in secrecy and placed with a family who is childless. The legacy of the family becomes disjointed and lost in this scenario.

What then is the answer for the present culture and its dilemma? What can be done to assure our safety if we continue on this downward slide toward depravity and sexual unaccountability and recklessness? One thing you can be sure of is that we are bound to find out because there is no escape if mankind is not willing to do the right thing as it was designed to be done. We will be without a defense. We will be sitting ducks, moving targets for the enemy of man who will continue to take our lives and impose the legal fines against us for the wrong that we do.

Perhaps, I will be given the honor of writing the answers to this dilemma, once men wake up to the need to find them. In the meantime, I encourage all men everywhere to look inside of themselves and to listen to the stillness. Is there a voice there?

What is it saying to you? What instructions about life are you receiving from outside of yourself, and which of those are you heeding rather than doing the good that is within you? As men continually sidestep the good to do evil, they will encounter the wrath of the enemy within. There is no escape but to choose to do good and avoid those who will do evil.

America must wake up, but so must the nations of the world who have embraced liberal doctrines of permissiveness and immorality. The conditions of those nations who embrace such things will only deteriorate. It is inevitable. There is no stopping the decline once the choices are made by those who serve in those nations to accept the bad behavior of men versus good. It is a downward spiral from this point for those who will not hear.

Let there then be an awakening of mankind to the inner nature of each of us. Let us be compelled to go in search of greater wisdom to do good for all men rather than to be in search of greater incivility individually and corporately, which can only harm one's self and those he knows.

It is time to change men and women, and that time is now. Will we heed the voice of reason or suffer the consequences of choosing recklessness over true freedom? I personally choose freedom, and my freedom has truly come.

Let the force be with you.